Mel Bay Presents

FRENCH MUSIC FOR ACCORDION

By Larry Hallar

CONTENTS

HISTORY OF THE MUSETTE

In the mid-1800's, the forerunners of the modern Accordion arrived in the Bastille district of Paris by train from the Auvergne. In fact, the rue de Lappe became a veritable Auvergne village in the heart of Paris. Since the Auvergnats were good tradesmen; setting up in business as scrap metal dealers and copper-smiths, opening cafés of all kinds (cafés-limonade, cafés-tabac and cafés-charbons); it was here that the waiters and waitresses from the small cafes, after their lunchtime duties, would get up and dance to the sound of the Auvergne musette (a small bagpipe called a cabrette), for a nominal charge of five centimes per dance. The bal-musette was born.

The Italians, on the other hand, arrived at the gare de Lyon. In their luggage was the accordion. Some establishments freely appropriated the bal-musette label, replacing the Auvergnat's cabrette with German or Italian instruments, replacing the bourrée with a free for all, and exchanging a jolly, good-time setting with the sinister atmosphere of the underworld. In 1887, in an effort to counter this trend, the Préfret de Police began to forbid the opening of any bal-musette which did not include authentic musette musicians.

Paris was the true stronghold of the musette, a far cry from the rowdy brasseries and country marquee dances. There were no brass instruments in the musette and children were not admitted. The dancers pursued their pleasure, attentively listening to the music. The musicians would set up on a platform, on a kind of balcony. The manager would take away the ladder, leaving them for hours playing above the heads of a "specialist audience," made up of expert dancers and connoisseurs of music. An expression of cosmopolitan Parisian life, the musette was as much an "affaire de style" as a melting-pot of other musical forms: songs, Latin and gypsy music...and swing.

Swing arrived on a boat from New York in the twenties and took France by storm, but it was not allowed in the bals-musette. This did not prevent Gus Viseur, Tony Murena and Jo Privat and their successors from playing jazz, whenever the occasion permitted, and spicing their waltzes with swing, a tendency strongly supported by the Gypsies. The gypsies lived on the outskirts of Paris, coming into the city to offer the services of their banjos and guitars, introducing the element of swing on these instruments for the first time.

The arrival of rock 'n roll signalled an end to this golden age. The style, the perfect rhythm and the wonderful gypsy accompaniment faded from view. The musette became identified with the sound of the accordion and its coarse vibration and wedding party repertoire. But, we couldn't let the popular Parisian culture languish. Therefore, Mel Bay presents this book of musette French music for the accordion.

LA CIGOULA
Paso Doble

Tony Murena
A. Baldi

D'LA VALSE DANS MA MUSETTE

Andre Verchuren
& Rene Denoncin

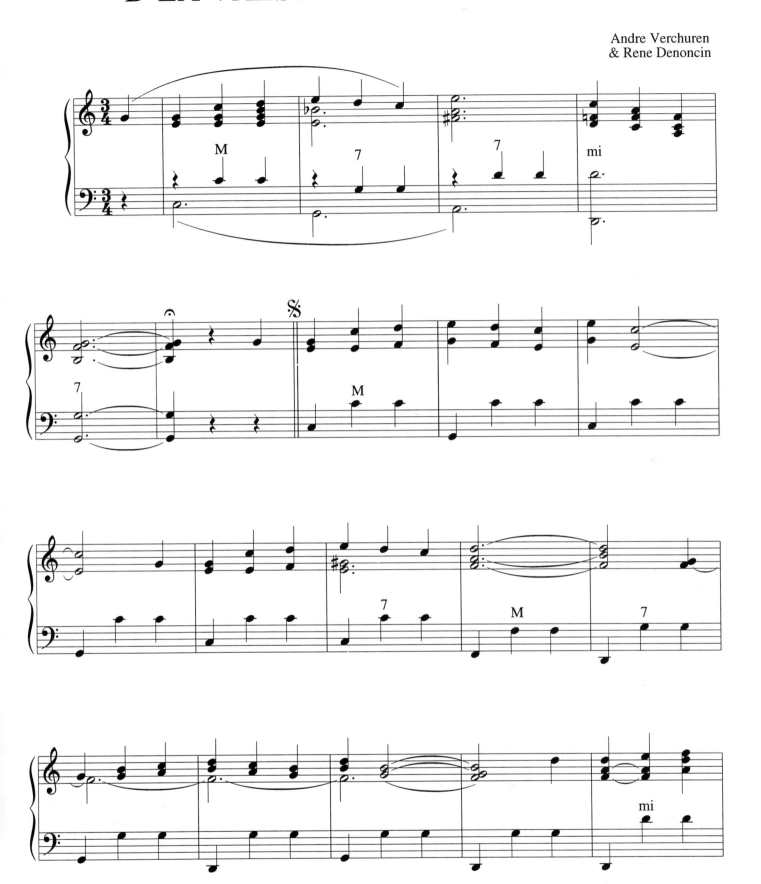

9

ACCORDÉON-SAMBA

Jean Peyronnin

D.S. ℅ al Trio

FUGITIVE

Valse

M. Ferrero

ALHAMBRA
Paso Doble

Albert Huard

ON DANSE A LA VILLETTE
Valse Musette

Emile
Carrara

D.S. ℅ al Fine

Fine

21

PERLES DE CRISTAL

Fantaisie Polka

Georges Hamel

ADIOS SEVILLA
Paso Doble

Tony Murena
& Jacques Chanzol

CALINERIE
Valse

Andre Verchuren

MA ROSE D'ALSACE

(Tango)

Robert Trabucco
& Maurice Denoux

BACK TO BACH
(Java)

Andre Paté
& Jacky Noguez

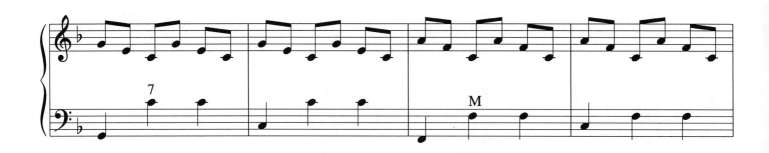

RAPID'
(Polka)

Fredo Gardoni

FANTAISIE POLKA

Jean Peyronnin
E. Prud' Homme

43

SEÑORITA ROSITA

Paso Doble

Jules Nicoli

ISULA DI SOGNU
(Ile de Rêve)

Bruno Lorenzoni

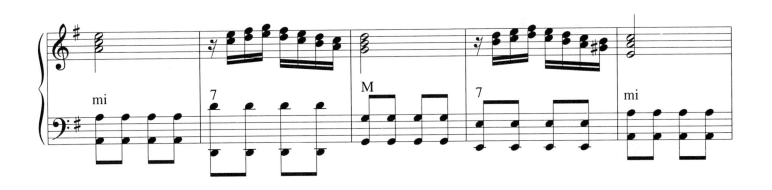

EN COUP DE VENT

Java

Albert Huard

Bass Solo

TROMPETTE - MUSETTE

Java Valse

Andre Verchuren
& Jo Moutet

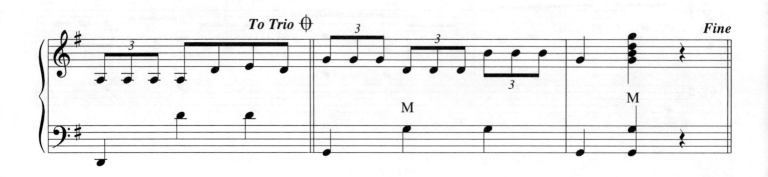

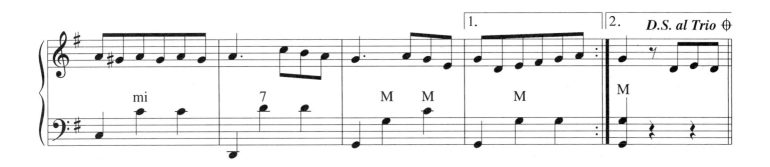

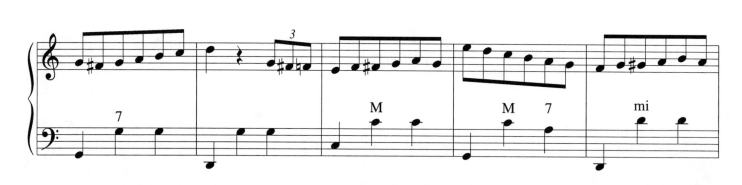

COMÈT' VALSE

Raymond
Siozade

57

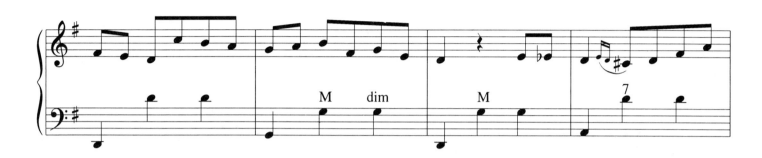

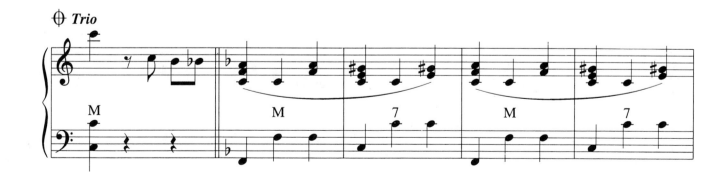

RADIO VALSE
Valse Brillante Pour Accordéon

Albert Huard
& S. Deplechin

LA GRANDE RONDE

Roberto Milesi

FLEUR DE PARIS
(Flower of Paris)

Henri Bourtayre

LES TEMPS FINIS

Jo Privat & Aimable

Intro

EUGÉNIE DE LA BASTILLE

Java

Jo Privat

ACCORDEÓN POLKA

Tony Murena
& Pascal Groffe

AU SOMMET DU CERVIN

Valse

Michel Geney
& José Marka